CONNECT BIBLE STUDIES

Madonna

Maverick/Warner Bros.

Materialism
Image
Family relationships
Spirituality

www.connectbiblestudies.com

connect

linking the Word to the world

CONNECT BIBLE STUDIES: Madonna

Published in this format by Scripture Union, 207–209 Queensway, Bletchley, MK2 2EB, England.
Scripture Union is an international Christian charity working with churches in more than 130 countries providing resources to bring the good news about Jesus Christ to children, young people and families – and to encourage them to develop spiritually through the Bible and prayer. As well as a network of volunteers, staff and associates who run holidays, church-based events and school Christian groups, Scripture Union produces a wide range of publications and supports those who use the resources through training programmes.
Email: info@scriptureunion.org.uk
Internet: www.scriptureunion.org.uk

© Damaris Trust, PO Box 200, Southampton, SO17 2DL.
Damaris Trust enables people to relate Christian faith and contemporary culture. It helps them to think about issues within society from a Christian perspective and explore God's truth as it is revealed in the Bible. Damaris provides resources via the Internet, workshops, publications and products.
Email: office@damaris.org
Internet: www.damaris.org

British Library Cataloguing-in-Publication Data: a catalogue record for this book is available from the British Library.
First published 2003 ISBN 1 84427 032 7

ALSO AVAILABLE AS AN ELECTRONIC DOWNLOAD: www.connectbiblestudies.com

Damaris writers: Di Archer, Tom Price, Caroline Puntis, Tony Watkins,
SU editors: Lin Ball, Andrew Clark

Cover design by aricot vert of Fleet, UK.

Print production by CPO, Garcia Estate, Canterbury Road, Worthing, West Sussex BN13 1BW.
CPO is a Christian publishing charity working in partnership with over 30,000 churches and other Christian organisations worldwide, using the power of design and print to convey the message of Jesus Christ. Established for over 45 years, CPO is the UK's premier supplier of publicity and related resources to the UK Church, available through a direct mail catalogue series, an e-commerce website and most Christian bookshops.
Email: connect@cpo.org.uk
Internet: www.cpo-online.org

Other titles in this series:

And more titles following. Check www.connectbiblestudies.com for latest titles or ask at any good Christian bookshop.

www.connectbiblestudies.com

connect
linking the Word to the world

Using Connect Bible Studies

What Are These Studies?

These innovative home group Bible studies have two aims. Firstly, to enable group members to dig into their Bibles and get to know them better. Secondly, by being based on contemporary films, books, TV programmes, music, etc., the aim is to help people think through topical issues in a biblical way.

It is not envisaged that all members will always be able to watch the films, play the music or read the books, or indeed that they will always want to. A summary is always provided. However, our vision is that knowing about these films and books empowers Christians to engage with friends and colleagues about them. Addressing issues from a Biblical perspective gives Christians confidence that they know what they think, and can bring a distinctive angle to bear in conversations.

The studies are produced in sets of four – i.e. four weeks' worth of group Bible Study material. These are available in print published by Scripture Union from your local Christian bookshop, or via the Internet: www.connectbiblestudies.com. Anyone can sign up for a free monthly email newsletter that announces the new studies and provides other information (sign up on the Connect Bible Studies website at www.connectbiblestudies.com/uk/register).

How Do I Use Them?

These studies are designed to stimulate creative thought and discussion within a Biblical context. Each section therefore has a range of questions or options from which you as leader may choose in order to tailor the study to your group's needs and desires. Different approaches may appeal at different times, so the studies aim to supply lots of choice. Whilst adhering to the main aim of corporate Bible study, some types of questions may enable this for your group better than others – so take your pick.

Group members should be supplied with the appropriate sheet that they can fill in, each one also showing the relevant summary.

Leader's notes contain:

1. Opening questions

These help your group settle in to discussion, while introducing the topics. They may be straightforward, personal or creative, but aim to provoke a response.

2. Summary

We suggest the summary of the book or film will follow now, read aloud if necessary. There may well be reactions that group members want to express even before getting on to the week's issue.

3. Key issue

Again, either read from the leader's notes, or summarise.

4. Bible study

Lots of choice here. Choose as appropriate to suit your group – get digging into the Bible. Background reading and texts for further help and study are suggested, but please use the material provided to inspire your group to explore their Bibles as much as possible. A concordance might be a handy standby for looking things up. A commentary could be useful too, such as the New Bible Commentary 21st century edition (IVP, 1994). The idea is to help people to engage with the truth of God's word, wrestling with it if necessary but making it their own.

Don't plan to work through every question here. Within each section the two questions explore roughly the same ground but from different angles or in different ways. Our advice is to take one question from each section. The questions are open-ended so each ought to yield good discussion – though of course any discussion in a Bible study may need prompting to go a little further.

5. Implications

Here the aim is to tie together the perspectives gained through Bible study and the impact of the book or film. The implications may be personal, a change in worldview, or new ideas for relating to non-churchgoers. Choose questions that adapt to the flow of the discussion.

6. Prayer

Leave time for it! We suggest a time of open prayer, or praying in pairs if the group would prefer. Encourage your members to focus on issues from your study that had a particular impact on them. Try different approaches to prayer – light a candle, say a prayer each, write prayers down, play quiet worship music – aiming to facilitate everyone to relate to God.

7. Background reading

You will find links to some background reading on the Connect Bible Studies website: www.connectbiblestudies.com/

8. Online Discussion

You can discuss the studies online with others on the Connect Bible Studies website at www.connectbiblestudies.com/discuss/

Scriptures referred to are taken from the Holy Bible, New International Version (NIV). Copyright © 1973, 1978, 1984 by International Bible Society. Other Bible translations can, of course, be used for the studies and having a range of translations in a group can be helpful and useful in discussion.

www.connectbiblestudies.com

connect
linking the Word to the world

Madonna

Maverick/Warner Bros.

Part One: Materialism

'Cause we are
Living in a material world
And I am a material girl
Material Girl, 1985

Please read Using Connect Bible Studies *(page 3) before leading a Bible study with this material.*

Opening Questions

Choose one of these questions.

	Do you like Madonna? Why/why not?	Why do you think Madonna is so successful?
	Does having lots of stuff mean you are successful? Why/why not?	Would you rather be rich or poor? Why?

Summary

Madonna has spent 20 years in the limelight. As an artist she has seen highs and lows, but at no point has her substantial personal fortune been in question. Unlike some of her contemporaries, she is not known for being frivolous with money: 'I'm not mean. I'm careful. I don't like to waste money. Just because you have money it doesn't mean you should go throwing it around' *(Friday Night with Jonathan Ross,* BBC, May 2003).

Nonetheless, Madonna claims that she has woken up from the 'American dream', and doesn't like what she sees. The message on her latest album, *American Life,* is serious throughout: 'It's me wanting to shout from the rooftops that we've all been living in a dream. We have to wake up to reality and realise that the physical world and the illusions of the material world are traps' *(Madonna Speaks,* VH1, May 2003).

In the pop industry, Madonna is regarded as an astute businesswoman. As *American Life* draws to a close, she voices her desire: 'I want the good life / But I don't want an easy ride / What I want is to work for it' *(Easy Ride)*. Madonna appears to be a product of the belief that you can have anything or be anyone if you work hard enough. She feels that she has every right to speak on the subject of fame and fortune, and has much to say on the cult of celebrity: 'It's the allure of the beautiful life. Look like this, you're gonna be happy. Drive this car, you're gonna be popular. Wear these clothes and people are gonna want to [have sex with] you. It's a very powerful illusion and people are caught up in it, including myself. Or I was' *(Q Magazine, May 2003)*.

Key Issue: Materialism

Early on in her career, Madonna appeared to lap up the material consequences of her success as a singer. Her song *Material Girl* extolled the virtues of a materialistic lifestyle, and she seemed to have all the 'stuff' she needed at her fingertips. However, *American Life* reveals a disillusionment with happiness through things and, as Christians, we know that 'having stuff' is not the answer to life. But what should our relationship towards material goods be? Is it wrong to have things? How can the Bible help us to get our perspective right?

Bible Study

Choose one question from each section.

1. Material success

> *I got a lawyer and a manager / An agent and a chef / Three nannies, an assistant / And a driver and a jet / A trainer and a butler / And a bodyguard or five / A gardener and a stylist / Do you think I'm satisfied?* (American Life, 2003)

- ◆ Read 2 Chronicles 9:1–12. Why was the Queen of Sheba so impressed by Solomon? What does the passage tell us about Solomon's relationships with God and with possessions?

- ◆ Read Luke 16:1–15. Put Jesus' interpretation of this parable into your own words. Why does Jesus' teaching cause the Pharisees to sneer at him?

2. Enjoying the material world

> *I drive my Mini Cooper / And I'm feeling super-dooper / ... And you know I'm satisfied* (American Life, 2003)

- ◆ Read 2 Chronicles 1:11,12 and 9:13–28. What was the source of Solomon's wealth? How did Solomon enjoy his riches?

◆ Read 2 Corinthians 9:6–15. How can we enjoy God's blessings with him? Why does Paul warn the Corinthians not to 'sow sparingly'?

3. Disillusionment – waking up

I'm just living out the American dream / And I just realised that nothing / Is what it seems (American Life, 2003)

◆ Read Ecclesiastes 5:10–17. Why was the writer disillusioned with wealth? What are the benefits of living a poor and simple life?

◆ Read Haggai 1:3–11. Why were the people disillusioned? What was God saying to them about their priorities?

4. Perspective – true satisfaction

I tried to stay ahead / I tried to stay on top / I tried to play the part / But somehow I forgot / Just what I did it for / And why I wanted more / This type of modern life / Is it for me? / This type of modern life / Is it for free? (American Life, 2003)

◆ Read Ecclesiastes 5:18–20. When should we be satisfied with our lot? How is this possible?

◆ Read Psalm 49:1–20. What are the dangers associated with being rich, according to the Psalmist? How does he put material wealth into perspective?

Implications

Please don't try to tempt me / It was just greed / And it won't protect me / Don't want my dreams / Adding up to nothing / I was just looking for / Everybody's looking for something
(I'm So Stupid, 2003)

Choose one or more of the following questions.

- ◆ Is there a limit to how much Christians should have?

- ◆ Do you measure your own or other people's worth by their bank balance? What is wrong with this, and how could you change?

- ◆ Is it easier or harder to be faithful to God in the prosperous times? Why?

- ◆ How much do you enjoy what God has given you, in terms of material wealth? Are you happy with your lot?

- ◆ To what extent do you put your trust in the material world? How could you rely on God more?

- ◆ Is there a Christian imperative to respond to the needs of the poor, especially those in the developing world? How do you feel about your response?

- ◆ What would you say to someone who envies Madonna's riches? What would you say to someone who thinks they have 'made it'?

- ◆ How might you use your money and possessions to grow the kingdom of God?

Prayer

Spend some time praying through these issues.

Background Reading

You will find links to some background reading on the Connect Bible Studies website: www.connectbiblestudies.com/uk/catalogue/0020/background.htm

Discuss

Discuss this study in the online discussion forums at www.connectbiblestudies.com/discuss

Members' Sheet: Madonna — Part 1

Summary

Madonna has spent 20 years in the limelight. As an artist she has seen highs and lows, but at no point has her substantial personal fortune been in question. Unlike some of her contemporaries, she is not known for being extravagant with money: 'I'm not mean. I'm careful. I don't like to waste money. Just because you have money it doesn't mean you should go throwing it around' *(Friday Night with Jonathan Ross,* BBC, May 2003).

Nonetheless, Madonna claims that she has woken up from the 'American dream', and doesn't like what she sees. The message on her latest album, *American Life,* is serious throughout: 'It's me wanting to shout from the rooftops that we've all been living in a dream. We have to wake up to reality and realise that the physical world and the illusions of the material world are traps' *(Madonna Speaks,* VH1, May 2003).

In the pop industry, Madonna is regarded as an astute businesswoman. As *American Life* draws to a close, she voices her desire: 'I want the good life / But I don't want an easy ride / What I want is to work for it' *(Easy Ride).* Madonna appears to be a product of the belief that you can have anything or be anyone if you work hard enough. She feels that she has every right to speak on the subject of fame and fortune, and has much to say on the cult of celebrity: 'It's the allure of the beautiful life. Look like this, you're gonna be happy. Drive this car, you're gonna be popular. Wear these clothes and people are gonna want to [have sex] with you. It's a very powerful illusion and people are caught up in it, including myself. Or I was' *(Q* Magazine, May 2003).

Key Issue

Bible Study notes

Implications

Prayer

connect

linking the Word to the world

Madonna

Maverick/Warner Bros.

Part Two: Image

Nobody knows me
Like you know me
Nobody Knows Me, 2003

Please read Using Connect Bible Studies *(page 3) before leading a Bible study with this material.*

Opening Questions

Choose one of these questions.

How have you reacted to Madonna's different images over the years?	Why do you think Madonna shocks people?
Does everyone have an image? Why/why not?	Does presenting an image of yourself mean you are being dishonest? Why/why not?

Summary

The ability to reinvent herself is Madonna's trademark. She says that she never wants to repeat herself, musically or otherwise. This attitude, combined with a desire to shock and express herself as an artist, has caused some explosive moments in the history of pop. In 1989 her promotional video for *Like A Prayer* caused a furore for its blend of eroticism and religion, causing a lucrative deal with Pepsi to collapse. In 1990, MTV refused to play her video promoting *Justify My Love*, which featured Madonna kissing another woman. Ironically, MTV chose to screen her much-publicised kisses with Britney Spears and Christina Aguilera from their 2003 Video Music Awards.

After she had bared all in her sell-out book *Sex* (1992), it may have looked to some that Madonna had nowhere left to go. But perhaps most shocking of all is her insistence that she has seen through the images she worked so hard to create. Her recent lyrics demonstrate a newfound awareness of herself, and the industry that she has dedicated her life to: 'Do I have to change my name? / Will it get me far? / Should I lose some weight? / Am I gonna be a star?'

(American Life). Her promotional videos are still controversial, but now the shockwaves are political. As the war with Iraq erupted, Madonna decided to withdraw her video for *American Life,* which showed her throwing a hand grenade into a fashion show.

She says, 'I'm not ashamed of who I was ten years ago ... I thought I was going to liberate all the women of the world ... Everyone changes and everyone grows – that's what happens to human beings. It's been an incredible ride, adventure, test – whatever you want to call it – only I don't want people to dress like me any more. I want them to think like me' *(Madonna Speaks,* VH1, May 2003).

Key Issue: Image

It is probably impossible to separate Madonna's music from her various images over the years. Many people have felt that she has 'gone too far', particularly with her sexual bravado, but also with her provocative religious images, which have been seen as blasphemous. She seemed to have no barriers when it came to what she would do or be, and people have loved or hated her for it. In this study we ask how the Bible can help us think through the issue of image and also the shock tactics Madonna has employed. In *American Life* Madonna seems to say that we do not know the real her. So can the Bible give us a true perspective on who we are?

Bible Study

Choose one question from each section. One question in each section is based on Luke's gospel – you may like to follow these throughout the study.

1. Image

Everybody comes to Hollywood / They wanna make it in the neighbourhood / They like the smell of it in Hollywood / How could it hurt you when it looks so good?
(Hollywood, 2003)

◆ Read Jeremiah 7:1–29. How were the people being deceptive? Why was God not impressed?

> *Leaders: God, through Jeremiah, was rebuking Israel for treating the temple with contempt. They believed it provided protection for the people, like a talisman. Shiloh was the location of the tabernacle and ark after the conquest of Canaan and throughout the time of the judges (Joshua 18:1). The Philistines captured the ark after Israel became idolatrous (1 Samuel 4:1–11) and probably destroyed Shiloh afterwards. Although there isn't an historical account of this in the Bible, archaeological findings confirm that it was desroyed around 1050 BC. See also Psalm 78:56–64.*

◆ Read Luke 4:1–13. Describe the image that Jesus was tempted to adopt. Why couldn't the devil succeed?

2. Controversy

'When I think of controversy, I never really think people are going to be half as shocked as they are at what I do. I really couldn't believe how out of control the whole Pepsi thing got.' (Madonna: Blonde Ambition, Mark Bego, 1992)

◆ Read Hosea 1:1–11; 3:1–5. How do you think the people would have responded to Hosea's actions? What truth did the Lord show the people about themselves?

◆ Read Luke 5:17–31. Why was Jesus controversial? What reactions did he provoke?

3. Disillusionment – image exposed

I'm so stupid / 'Cause I used to live / In a tiny bubble / And I wanted to be / Like all the pretty people / That were all around me / But now I know for sure / That I was stupid (I'm So Stupid, 2003)

◆ Read 2 Samuel 24:1–25. How was David foolish? How did God deal with him?

Leaders: The parallel passage (1 Chronicles 21:1–17) attributes the inciting of David to Satan rather than the Lord. 2 Samuel 24 must be referring to the 'permissive will' of God. In other words, the Lord is angry with Israel and therefore allows Satan to incite David to take a census.

◆ Read Luke 6:37–49. How does Jesus challenge the way we see others, and ourselves, in this passage? Does image have a place in the kingdom of God? Why?

4. Perspective – in God's eyes

But why should I care / What the world thinks of me? / Won't let a stranger / Give me a social disease / I don't want no lies / I don't watch TV / I don't waste my time / Won't read a magazine (Nobody Knows Me, 2003)

◆ Read Psalm 139:1–24. How did David see himself in relation to God? What perspective does this psalm bring to our self-image?

◆ Read Luke 7:36–50. How might the other guests have changed their views of Simon, Jesus and the woman during this meal? How did Jesus challenge Simon the Pharisee's perspective?

Implications

This world is not so kind / People trap your mind / It's so hard to find / Someone to admire
(*Nobody Knows Me*, 2003)

Choose one or more of the following questions.

◆   Is controversy always bad? How do you respond to controversy in your church?

◆   How can we be true to ourselves and less dependent on image? What holds us back from being who we really are? How can we help each other in this?

◆   As Christians, should we always be 'nice'? Are there times when we should be controversial? Can we be both?

◆   Have you ever been shocked by God?

◆   How do you think God sees you? Are you willing for God to change the way you see others and yourself? How could this happen?

◆   What would you say to someone who is impressed by Madonna's frequent image changes?

◆   What does our response to Madonna's shock tactics say about our society?

◆   Is there something in you that would like to be famous? What is the appeal? Are there ways that we try to be celebrities in our own circles?

Prayer

Spend some time praying through these issues.

Background Reading

You will find links to some background reading on the Connect Bible Studies website:
www.connectbiblestudies.com/uk/catalogue/0020/background.htm

Discuss

Discuss this study in the online discussion forums at www.connectbiblestudies.com/discuss

Members' Sheet: Madonna — Part 2

Summary

The ability to reinvent herself is Madonna's trademark. She says that she never wants to repeat herself, musically or otherwise. This attitude, combined with a desire to shock and express herself as an artist, has caused some explosive moments in the history of pop. In 1989 her promotional video for *Like A Prayer* caused a furore for its blend of eroticism and religion, causing a lucrative deal with Pepsi to collapse. In 1990, MTV refused to play her video promoting *Justify My Love*, which featured Madonna kissing another woman. Ironically, MTV chose to screen her much-publicised kisses with Britney Spears and Christina Aguilera from their 2003 Video Music Awards.

After she had bared all in her sell-out book *Sex* (1992), it may have looked to some that Madonna had nowhere left to go. But perhaps most shocking of all is her insistence that she has seen through the images she worked so hard to create. Her recent lyrics demonstrate a newfound awareness of herself, and the industry that she has dedicated her life to: 'Do I have to change my name? / Will it get me far? / Should I lose some weight? / Am I gonna be a star?' *(American Life)*. Her promotional videos are still controversial, but now the shockwaves are political. As the war with Iraq erupted, Madonna decided to withdraw her video for *American Life,* which showed her throwing a hand grenade into a fashion show.

She says, 'I'm not ashamed of who I was ten years ago ... I thought I was going to liberate all the women of the world ... Everyone changes and everyone grows – that's what happens to human beings. It's been an incredible ride, adventure, test – whatever you want to call it – only I don't want people to dress like me any more. I want them to think like me' *(Madonna Speaks,* VH1, May 2003).

Key Issue

Bible Study notes

Implications

Prayer

connect

linking the Word to the world

Madonna

Maverick/Warner Bros.

Part Three: Family Relationships

Cherish the thought
Of always having you here by my side
Cherish, 1989

Please read Using Connect Bible Studies _(page 3) before leading a Bible study with this material._

Opening Questions

Choose one of these questions.

Do you have a favourite Madonna track? Why do you like it?	What is your most important relationship and why does it matter to you?
Define 'family'.	What are the most important features of a good relationship for you?

Summary

Mother and Father, from _American Life_ (2003), is not Madonna's first attempt to exorcise the demons of her childhood. 1995 saw the release of _Oh Father,_ a testimony to how she overcame the pain she endured at her father's hands: 'Maybe someday / When I look back I'll be able to say / You didn't mean to be cruel / Somebody hurt you too'. In 1998, on _Mer Girl,_ she wrote of how she felt haunted by her dead mother. Now she adds, 'Oh mother why aren't you here with me? / No one else saw the things that you could see / I'm trying hard to dry my tears / Yes father you know I'm not so free'.

In 1996 Madonna gave birth to her first child, Lourdes, then later had a son, Rocco. Evidently, motherhood has had a profound effect on Madonna's values and her self-perception: 'I find they help me see myself and my own weaknesses because I see my daughter reacting in a certain way ... Your children really are mirrors of you, they're sparks of your soul' (_Madonna Speaks,_ VH1, May 2003).

But it is her relationship with film director Guy Ritchie that seems to have affected Madonna's music the most. She says, 'I knew that Guy was the right person in five minutes ... It's a deep connection. We have a great level of honesty and communication' (*Madonna Speaks,* VH1, May 2003). Her love songs have acquired a new joy since they got together in 1998. 'For the first time in my life, I'm in a real family rather than pining for one. My children are amazing, thank God. My husband is amazing. To a certain extent, they have grounded me, but if I wasn't studying Kabbalah* I most likely might have screwed those up' (usatoday.com).

*a brand of Jewish mysticism (see Part 4)

Key Issue: Family relationships

Madonna makes no secret of the fact that losing her mother when she was five was very hard for her, or that her relationship with her father has not been ideal. Many of us would identify with Madonna in this – none of us come from perfect families or backgrounds. Perhaps this is one reason why Madonna's lyrics strike a chord with people. While she can express her emotions through singing, for practical help with family relationships we can turn to the Bible. Madonna has now found contentment in her husband and children. For us, whether it is family, or best friends and loving communities, what does the Bible say about cherishing our good relationships?

Bible Study

Choose one question from each section.

1. The impact of childhood

There was a time I had a mother it was nice / Nobody else would ever take the place of you / Nobody else could do the things that you could do (Mother and Father, 2003)

◆ Read 2 Chronicles 22:1–4; 1 Kings 22:51–53; 2 Chronicles 26:1–8; 2 Chronicles 17:3-6. What and who were significant in the lives of the kings? What were the consequences?

> Leaders: The Ahaziah mentioned in 1 Kings 22:51–53 is not the same as the one in 2 Chronicles 22:1–4. The first was king of the northern kingdom, Israel; the second was king of the southern kingdom, Judah.

◆ Read 2 Timothy 1:5; 3:14, 15; Matthew 14:6–12. Why were the family relationships important? What were the consequences?

2. Disillusionment – with family

My father had to go to work / I used to think he was a jerk / I didn't know his heart was broken / And not another word was spoken / He became a shadow of / The father I was dreaming of (Mother and Father, 2003)

◆ Read 1 Samuel 20:1–11, 24–34. How did Saul let Jonathan down? Why did they both get so angry?

Leaders: David had been popular with Saul for a brief time, but Saul soon gave in to jealousy of David's superior gifts. Saul was convinced David was a rival to his throne and wanted to kill him. David agreed with Jonathan that he would hide in a field during the New Moon festival while Jonathan found out if David was really in danger.

◆ Read Ephesians 6:1–9. What difference does being 'in the Lord' make to family relationships? What impact can children and parents have on each other?

3. Perspective – loving and being loved

I got to give it up / Find someone to love me / I got to let it go / Find someone that I can care for (Mother and Father, 2003)

◆ Read Song of Songs 8:5–7. What do each of the metaphors express about the nature of the relationship?

◆ Read 1 Corinthians 12:31b–13:13. Why is love 'the most excellent way'?

4. Celebrating children

'Being in the entertainment business means having a tendency – we all do – to become incredibly self-obsessed. You live in front of the camera and there's the exercising, the clothes, the hair, the nails ... it just goes on and on – and then you have children and there's no time. It's the best thing that could happen because it throws everything into perspective.' (Madonna Speaks, VH1, May 2003)

◆ Read Genesis 17:1–27. How did God plan to fulfil his covenant with Abraham? What was Abraham's responsibility?

◆ Read Luke 18:15–17. How did Jesus celebrate children? What do they teach us about the kingdom?

Implications

I made a vow that I would never need another person ever / Turned my heart into a cage, a victim of a kind of rage (Mother and Father, 2003)

Choose one or more of the following questions. We are dealing with potentially painful subjects, so extra sensitivity might be needed.

◆ How can you cherish the good relationships in your life?

◆ What does love mean to you? How do you best receive and give love?

◆ Do you have difficult memories from your childhood? How could you allow God to bring his healing to you?

◆ What would you say to someone who thinks having a child would interrupt a fulfilling life?

◆ Do you know someone who has lost a family member recently? How could you care for them more?

◆ How can we show sensitivity to and care for each other, no matter what our family status is?

◆ Do you need to forgive/contact/help/celebrate members of your family?

Prayer

Spend some time praying through these issues.

Background Reading

You will find links to some background reading on the Connect Bible Studies website: www.connectbiblestudies.com/uk/catalogue/0020/background.htm

Discuss

Discuss this study in the online discussion forums at www.connectbiblestudies.com/discuss

Members' Sheet: Madonna — Part 3

Summary

Mother and Father, from *American Life* (2003), is not Madonna's first attempt to exorcise the demons of her childhood. 1995 saw the release of *Oh Father,* a testimony to how she overcame the pain she endured at her father's hands: 'Maybe someday / When I look back I'll be able to say / You didn't mean to be cruel / Somebody hurt you too'. In 1998, on *Mer Girl,* she wrote of how she felt haunted by her dead mother. Now she adds, 'Oh mother why aren't you here with me? / No one else saw the things that you could see / I'm trying hard to dry my tears / Yes father you know I'm not so free'.

In 1996 Madonna gave birth to her first child, Lourdes, then later had a son, Rocco. Evidently, motherhood has had a profound effect on Madonna's values and her self-perception: 'I find they help me see myself and my own weaknesses because I see my daughter reacting in a certain way ... Your children really are mirrors of you, they're sparks of your soul' *(Madonna Speaks,* VH1, May 2003).

But it is her relationship with film director Guy Ritchie that seems to have affected Madonna's music the most. She says, 'I knew that Guy was the right person in five minutes ... It's a deep connection. We have a great level of honesty and communication' *(Madonna Speaks,* VH1, May 2003). Her love songs have acquired a new joy since they got together in 1998. 'For the first time in my life, I'm in a real family rather than pining for one. My children are amazing, thank God. My husband is amazing. To a certain extent, they have grounded me, but if I wasn't studying Kabbalah* I most likely might have screwed those up' (usatoday.com).

*a brand of Jewish mysticism (see Part 4)

Key Issue

Bible Study notes

Implications

Prayer

connect

linking the Word to the world

Madonna

Maverick/Warner Bros.

Part Four: Spirituality

When you call my name it's like a little prayer
Like A Prayer, 1989

Please read Using Connect Bible Studies *(page 3) before leading a Bible study with this material.*

Opening Questions

Choose one of these questions.

Are you surprised that Madonna is interested in spirituality? Why/why not?	Is our society spiritual? Why/why not?
Is there a difference between being spiritual and being religious? If so, what is it?	Is everyone spiritual? Why/why not?

Summary

Madonna was brought up in the Roman Catholic faith. She spent her formative years in a Catholic high school, which produced all kinds of rebellion. When she left to pursue her dream of becoming a performer she took the imagery with her, but not the lifestyle. Madonna put faith in herself, working steadily to build a successful and influential career.

After more than a decade of worshipping the material, she turned to the spiritual practice of Kabbalah for some answers to the questions she had about life. Attracted by the way people accepted her for who she really was, rather than for her status as a pop icon, Madonna became a serious student of Kabbalah. The ancient teachings describe how the universe operates in relation to the Creator, and how people can only achieve fulfilment in life through an understanding of its spiritual laws. 'It is a precise description of the interwoven nature of spiritual and physical reality – and it is a full complement of powerful, practical methods for attaining worthy goals within that reality' (kabbalah.com).

Followers of Kabbalah each wear a red piece of string that has been in contact with the tomb of Jacob's wife Rachel, their spiritual mother. These wristbands are said to ward off negative thoughts. Madonna is confident that her search for truth is over: 'I have the answer, yes. We're here to share, to give, to love. When you die your physical body no longer exists, but your soul, and what you gave, how you loved, goes with you. I believe in reincarnation and ultimately that we are all united' (Q Magazine, May 2003). Kabbalah is also the inspiration for Madonna's series of children's books, launched in September 2003 with *The English Roses.*

Key Issue: Spirituality

At one time, Madonna was shocking people in her music video by kissing a crucified Christ. Now she is embracing Kabbalah, a brand of Jewish mysticism. It seems she has been asking questions about spirituality for a while, but has firmly rejected her Catholic background. Most of us know about spiritual confusion and the search for truth, so what does the Bible say about them? What about those who, like Madonna, find answers elsewhere? Her main conviction seems to be that love is supreme. How does that fit with the truth of the Bible?

Bible Study

Choose one question from each section.

1. Questions

There are too many options / There is no consolation / I have lost my illusions / What I want is an explanation *(Love Profusion, 2003)*

◆   Read Job 10:1–22. What is Job expressing in his questions? What do they reveal about Job and his understanding of God?

◆   Read Luke 18:18–30. What do the ruler's question – and his responses to Jesus – show us about him? What does Jesus reveal about the kingdom of God in the ensuing discussion?

2. Rejecting religion

'I don't think there's anything wrong with the teachings of Jesus, but I am suspicious of organised religion. Kabbalah has nothing to do with organised religion. It's not judgmental. It's a manual for living.' (usatoday.com)

◆   Read Deuteronomy 32:15–43. In what ways did Israel reject God? Trace the progression of God's response.

Leaders: This passage starts halfway through a poem – the Song of Moses. The first part talks about the way God has provided everything for Israel. Jeshurun means 'the upright one', and in this context refers to Israel.

◆   Read 1 Peter 2:4–12. What is the price of rejection? How does the way Jesus was rejected benefit us?

3. Disillusionment – confusion

There are too many questions / There is not one solution / There is no resurrection / There is so much confusion (Love Profusion, 2003)

- ◆ Read Ezekiel 8:1–18. What evidence did Ezekiel see of the religious confusion in Israel? Why are these things detestable to God?

    Leaders: Ezekiel was in exile in Babylon. This passage describes the first part of a vision in which God shows Ezekiel the nature of the idolatry back home in Jerusalem.

- ◆ Read 2 Timothy 2:14–3:9. What does Paul see as the consequences of false teaching? How are we to respond?

    Leaders: It is important to realise that 2:14–3:9 forms one section of this letter to Timothy. Note that Paul was not accusing women in general of being weak-willed, but rather saying that those women who were weak-willed were particularly vulnerable.

4. Perspective – love is the answer

I'm not religious / But I feel so moved / Makes me want to pray / Pray you'll always be here (Nothing Fails, 2003)

- ◆ Read Hosea 11:1–11. How does God love Israel (Ephraim)? What other aspects of God's character are described in this passage?

- ◆ Read 1 John 4:7–21. According to John, how do we know about God's love? How does it transform a Christian's life?

Implications

There is no comprehension / There is real isolation / There is so much destruction / What I want is a celebration (Love Profusion, 2003)

Choose one or more of the following questions.

- What questions are you asking of God and life at the moment? What do they reveal about who you are, and what you struggle with?

- Do you get angry with God? Do you tell him? Why/why not?

- Do you see God as passionate? ... About you? Why/why not?

- What would you say to someone who agrees with Madonna – that love is the answer to life?

- What would you say to a friend who says God cannot possibly be a God of love because they lost a parent as a child?

- How would you describe the religious confusion in our culture? How can you respond to it?

- How can you experience more of God's love for you? How can you love him more?

Prayer
Spend some time praying through these issues.

Background Reading
You will find links to some background reading on the Connect Bible Studies website: www.connectbiblestudies.com/uk/catalogue/0020/background.htm

Discuss
Discuss this study in the online discussion forums at www.connectbiblestudies.com/discuss

Summary

Madonna was brought up in the Roman Catholic faith. She spent her formative years in a Catholic high school, which produced all kinds of rebellion. When she left to pursue her dream of becoming a performer she took the imagery with her, but not the lifestyle. Madonna put faith in herself, working steadily to build a successful and influential career.

After more than a decade of worshipping the material, she turned to the spiritual practice of Kabbalah for some answers to the questions she had about life. Attracted by the way people accepted her for who she really was, rather than for her status as a pop icon, Madonna became a serious student of Kabbalah. The ancient teachings describe how the universe operates in relation to the Creator, and how people can only achieve fulfilment in life through an understanding of its spiritual laws. 'It is a precise description of the interwoven nature of spiritual and physical reality – and it is a full complement of powerful, practical methods for attaining worthy goals within that reality' (kabbalah.com).

Followers of Kabbalah each wear a red piece of string that has been in contact with the tomb of Jacob's wife Rachel, their spiritual mother. These wristbands are said to ward off negative thoughts. Madonna is confident that her search for truth is over: 'I have the answer, yes. We're here to share, to give, to love. When you die your physical body no longer exists, but your soul, and what you gave, how you loved, goes with you. I believe in reincarnation and ultimately that we are all united' (Q Magazine, May 2003). Kabbalah is also the inspiration for Madonna's series of children's books, launched in September 2003 with The English Roses.

Key Issue

Bible Study notes

Implications

Prayer